IMAGES OF WAR

6TH SS MOUNTAIN DIVISION NORD AT WAR 1941-1945

RARE PHOTOGRAPHS FROM WARTIME ARCHIVES

Ian Baxter

Pen & Sword
MILITARY

First published in Great Britain in 2019 by
PEN & SWORD MILITARY
An imprint of
Pen & Sword Books Ltd
47 Church Street
Barnsley
South Yorkshire
S70 2AS

ISBN 978-1-52672-138-9

A CIP catalogue record for this book is available from the British Library.

Typeset by Concept, Huddersfield, West Yorkshire HD4 5JL.
Printed and bound in England by CPI Group (UK) Ltd, Croydon CR0 4YY.

Pen & Sword Books Limited incorporates the imprints of Atlas, Archaeology, Aviation, Discovery, Family History, Fiction, History, Maritime, Military, Military Classics, Politics, Select, Transport, True Crime, Air World, Frontline Publishing, Leo Cooper, Remember When, Seaforth Publishing, The Praetorian Press, Wharncliffe Local History, Wharncliffe Transport, Wharncliffe True Crime and White Owl.

For a complete list of Pen & Sword titles please contact
PEN & SWORD BOOKS LIMITED
47 Church Street, Barnsley, South Yorkshire S70 2AS, England
E-mail: enquiries@pen-and-sword.co.uk
Website: www.pen-and-sword.co.uk

Contents

About the Author

Ian Baxter is a military historian who specialises in German twentieth century military history. He has written more than fifty books including *Poland – The Eighteen Day Victory March, Panzers In North Africa, The Ardennes Offensive, The Western Campaign, The 12th SS Panzer-Division Hitlerjugend, The Waffen-SS on the Western Front, The Waffen-SS on the Eastern Front, The Red Army at Stalingrad, Elite German Forces of World War II, Armoured Warfare, German Tanks of War, Blitzkrieg, Panzer-Divisions at War, Hitler's Panzers, German Armoured Vehicles of World War Two, Last Two Years of the Waffen-SS at War, German Soldier Uniforms and Insignia, German Guns of the Third Reich, Defeat to Retreat: The Last Years of the German Army At War 1943–45, Operation Bagration – the Destruction of Army Group Centre, German Guns of the Third Reich, Rommel and the Afrika Korps, U-Boat War,* and most recently *The Sixth Army and the Road to Stalingrad*. He has written over a hundred articles including 'Last days of Hitler', 'Wolf's Lair', 'The Story of the V1 and V2 Rocket Programme', 'Secret Aircraft of World War Two', 'Rommel at Tobruk', 'Hitler's War With his Generals', 'Secret British Plans to Assassinate Hitler', 'The SS at Arnhem', 'Hitlerjugend', 'Battle of Caen 1944', 'Gebirgsjäger at War', 'Panzer Crews', 'Hitlerjugend Guerrillas', 'Last Battles in the East', 'The Battle of Berlin', and many more. He has also reviewed numerous military studies for publication, supplied thousands of photographs and important documents to various publishers and film production companies worldwide, and lectures to various schools, colleges and universities throughout the United Kingdom and the Republic of Ireland.

Introduction

Drawing on a superb collection of rare and unpublished photographs, *6th SS Mountain Division Nord at War 1941–1945* is the sixth book in the popular series charting the Waffen-SS divisional history. This book tells the story of the 6th SS Mountain Division Nord, which was a German unit of the Waffen-SS formed in February 1941 as SS Kampfgruppe Nord (SS Battle Group North). The division was the only Waffen-SS unit to fight in the Arctic Circle when it was stationed in Finland and northern Russia between June and November 1941. It fought in the the Arctic Circle until September 1944, at which point it left Finland. The division saw extensive action in the Nordwind Operation in January 1945, where it suffered heavy losses. In early April 1945, the division was destroyed by US forces near Büdingen, Germany.

6th SS Nord Arctic Circle
1941–1944
Murmansk
Kantalahti
Salla
Kiestinki-Loui
Kestenga
NORWAY
FINLAND
RUSSIA
Lake
Onega
Lake
Ladoga
Helsinki
Leningrad
ARMY GROUP
NORD
© Lilly Corner

Chapter One

The Eastern Front 1941

During the early part of the war the SS-Verfügungstruppe had proved themselves beyond all expectations. They had fought with distinction not only in attack, but also with fanatical determination and gallantry even when greatly outnumbered and when other units had withdrawn. As a result of its reputation and success on the battlefield, it had expanded from one Waffen-SS division to five in less than a year. However, as the war against Russia loomed, further large-scale recruitment continued. This included yet another new SS-Kampfgruppe being formed and added to the already growing list of SS units.

For this new Kampfgruppe the men were initially drafted from ranks of the concentration camp guards, or SS-Totenkopfverbände, and formed into what was known as SS-Kampfgruppe Nord. Later this new SS unit began recruiting more men, mainly volunteers from Hungary, Romania and a few Norwegians, all built around a German cadre.

The SS-Kampfgruppe Nord's first duties were to guard the border with Russia in February 1941 following the German occupation of Norway in 1940. Two months later, in the spring of 1941, the Kampfgruppe, now with two new Standarten (regiments) comprising of mainly the 6th and 7th, was moved into positions at Salla in northern Finland under the command of General Nikolaus von Falkenhorst. Falkenhorst had been ground commander for the invasion of Norway and knew the territory well. SS-Kampfgruppe Nord consisted of a number of Totenkopfstandarten, containing military-age members of Allgemeine-SS which were transferred to Norway for garrison duties.

Many of the soldiers in Nord were untried in battle and their background as former concentration camp guards did little to induce confidence in the Wehrmacht. Even Falkenhorst himself did not trust their fighting ability. They were poorly equipped and not very well trained.

When the invasion of Russia finally came on 22 June 1941, Nord, which was part of Army Group North, was given the objective of striking through Finland into Russia to take the port of Murmansk in support of German Wehrmacht units. During its advance the SS-Kampfgruppe was thrown in the battle at Markajarvi-Salla in Operation Arctic Fox. The objective of Arctic Fox was to capture the town of Salla and then to advance in the direction of Kandalaksha with the intention of blocking the railway route to Murmansk. The operation was a joint attack by German and Finnish troops, combining experienced Finnish arctic troops and relatively unsuitable German forces from Norway including the Nord Kampfgruppe which was attached to the Norwegian Army with a unit strength of 9,505 men.

When the Fox operation was finally unleashed across much of the front Nord was confronted by a wall of flame and smoke. Soviet guns and mortars poured fire and destruction onto the SS regiments as they pushed forward. Shell after shell thundered into the German strongpoints. In the fields and forests surrounding Salla, Nord appeared to hold better than in the approaches towards the town. Here in the fields Red Army defences were destroyed, but still at a heavy cost in men.

In front of Nord, Russian artillery devoted most of its time to supporting the reconnaissance attacks and pulverising the German positions. During the assault on Salla, the men of SS-Nord, fearing complete annihilation, panicked, abandoned their weapons, and ran from the battlefield. In two days of fighting around Salla the Nord regiments had suffered huge losses. Falkenhorst was disappointed and angry that his men had abandoned their positions, and to him and his fellow German officers this was evidence that for racial and ideological reasons foreign soldiers did not make good troops.

In spite of the losses, German and Finnish units managed to capture the town of Salla. But German forces were unable to overcome the old pre-war Soviet border fortifications further east. The Finnish units on the other hand were able to make better progress, and came to within nineteen miles of the Murmansk railway. Yet again, strong Russian reinforcements prevented any further advance. The German front stagnated, and because of the situation further south in Central Russia, German commanders were unwilling to assign more men and equipment to the northern theatre, and called an end to their offensive.

Further south in Army Group North, German forces were making better ground. While the Luftwaffe dived and bombed, on the ground German artillery pounded the Soviet trench lines, to a depth of more than three miles in some places. Heavy artillery preparation lasted one to two hours on average, in some areas longer. As for the attacking German infantry, they were supported by a rolling barrage which continued unabated until the troops had succeeded in capturing the Russian defences.

Over the next days and weeks while Nord licked its wounds, infantry and Panzers of Army Group North attacked and bulldozed their way across northern Russia. Their strategic goal was Leningrad, with operational objectives being the territories of the Baltic States and securing the northern flank of Army Group Centre in northern Russia between the western Dvina River and the Daugavpils–Kholm line.

But Army Group North was losing momentum. Their supply lines being over-stretched and enemy resistance began to stiffen on the road to Leningrad. In front of the imperial city German troops became entangled in hundreds of miles of earth walls, anti-tank ditches, wire barricades, thousands of defensive pill-boxes, and the harrying activities of Russian tanks.

Further north, a replenished Kampfgruppe Nord, which had received some 700 Waffen-SS troop replacements, had been attached to the Finnish III Corps operating in the Kiestinki area. Fighting in the region had been moderate and losses to the SS regiments minimal.

In September 1941 the Kampfgruppe was redesignated as a division and subsequently renamed as the SS Gebirgs Division Nord (SS Mountain Division North). The order had come directly from Hitler: 'As for the SS-units, there is to be formed a new SS-Gebirgsbrigade formed by volunteering Norwegians and Finns. An Austrian SS-Regiment is to be attached, and the remaining units are to be deployed from Kampfgruppe Nord.' The division was now officially designated SS Division Nord and was handed over to the well-respected Finnish commander General Hjalmar Siilasvuo.

In November, SS Division Nord together with Wehrmacht and Finnish troops participated in a final drive towards the Murmansk railway in the last phase of Operation Arctic Fox. The troops again met with strong Russian resistance. General Siilasvuo soon realised that neither the Finnish nor the German high command was going to provide him with additional forces or substantial reinforcements to advance, so he slowed down his eastern advance and instead concentrated on clearing and securing the area. These mop-up operations were completed by 13 November. By that point the Finnish 3rd Division had killed 3,000 Soviet soldiers and captured 2,600.

It was here in the forests along the Kiestinki–Louhi road in November and December 1941 that Nord began conducting long-range patrols, raids against partisans and static combat against multiple Russian defences.

(**Above**) Seen here during a training exercise in the spring of 1941 are Nord and Gebirgsjäger troops with a PaK35/36 anti-tank gun. The PaK35/36 became the standard anti-tank gun for both the Heer and the Waffen-SS during the early part of the war. It weighed only 432kg and had a sloping splinter shield. The gun fired a solid shot round at a muzzle velocity of 2,500ft/s to a maximum range of 13,200 feet. Though these guns were effective against armour in Poland and the western front, it would not be until the war against Russia that the Germans became aware of its limitations as it increasingly encountered heavier enemy armour.

(**Opposite, above**) Stretcher bearers during a training exercise in the spring of 1941. It appears the men are training for a gas attack and can be seen with their gas masks at the ready.

(**Opposite, below**) During the opening phase of the invasion of Russia in the early summer of 1941, a Nord soldier during a reconnaissance mission can be seen surveying the terrain ahead with a pair of 6 × 30 binoculars.

A Flak soldier estimates the range to target with his EM34 optical range-finder. Should the rounds fall short or beyond the target, his task was to advise the Flak-aimer on the corrections needed for the battery to hit the target.

A Nord soldier cautiously moves forward, probably during a reconnaissance mission. Smoke can be seen rising into the air, giving a good indication of the enemy's location.

Soldiers of the Nord Division seen on the march in Army Group North. Resistance in this sector of the front was often fierce with the division sustaining heavy losses. Despite the casualties, the division managed to hold its line.

A long column of Opel Blitz supply trucks carrying infantry and equipment to the front. A flak gun can be seen on the road, either to defend the column against aerial attack, or as part of a defensive position from an earlier offensive operation. The divisional insignia of the Nord Division (the Hagal rune) is painted in on the mudguard of the second supply vehicle. The Hagal rune is the 'mother rune' in a system invented by the Austrian/German writer and mystic Guido von List (1848–1919), author of *The Secret Runes*. The word Hagal is sometimes wrongly confused with the German word 'Hagel' (hail stones) – the symbol used by Division Nord has nothing to do with hail.

(**Opposite, above**) A column of horse-drawn troops of the Nord Division pass a well camouflaged stationary Pz.Kpfw.III on a road somewhere in northern Russia. Nord was the only SS unit to fight in the Arctic Circle when it was stationed in Finland and northern Russia between June and November 1941.

(**Opposite, below**) A motorcycle combination follows a Kleiner Panzerbefehlswagen (a command vehicle converted from the obsolete Pz.Kpfw.I chassis by removing the turret and substituting an armoured box-like structure) along a typical Russian road in Army Group North. Troops of the Nord Division can be seen lining either side of the road during what appears to be a pause in their march.

(**Above**) Along a congested road full of vehicles belonging to the Nord Division, SS troops can be seen using a ditch as cover, probably in order to avoid enemy aerial recognition. Note the Hagal rune of the Nord Division on the rear of the cross-country vehicle.

A good photograph showing an SS Nord troop leader in a posed shot. He is wearing a summer camouflage smock, a pair of Zeiss 6 × 30 binoculars, and is armed with a captured Russian PPSh-41 machine gun. The PPSh was a magazine-fed sub-machine gun using open bolt blowback action. The weapon could be loaded with either a box or drum magazine and fired the 7.62 × 25mm Tokarev pistol round. During the war both the Heer and the Waffen-SS used these captured Russian guns extensively, even on the western front in 1944.

(**Opposite, above**) Troops of the 1 Kompanie Regiment 11 of the Division Nord are seen manhandling a PaK35/36 anti-tank gun along a road during an offensive operation. The gun was carried on a two-wheel split-trail carriage of tubular construction with a small sloped splinter shield. A well concealed anti-tank position was capable of causing some serious damage to its enemy. During early operations in northern Russia the Pak35/36 was not used extensively as there was limited armoured opposition.

(**Opposite, below**) Troops can be seen laughing and joking in one of the many positions along the front in the summer of 1941. The position appears to be out in the open, and Zeltbahn shelter quarters have been erected to help protect the men from the elements and enemy detection. Note that foliage from surrounding trees has helped conceal their camp. Behind them, a light Horch cross-country vehicle has also been camouflaged with saplings.

Commanding officers can be seen out in the field. The man on the left is a SS-Unterscharführer, the soldier in the middle is a SS-Sturmbannführer, while the man on the right holds the rank of a SS-Oberscharführer.

A blurred photograph showing a column of support vehicles belonging to Division Nord on the march in the summer of 1941 in northern Russia.

Tank men can be seen during a pause in the divisional unit's march in 1941. The tank is a Pz.Kpfw.III Ausf.J armed with the KwK 38 L/42 gun. The co-axial MG34 was a standard fitting on all German tanks for both offensive and defensive purposes.

A commanding officer pictured on the right confers with two infantrymen and the officer's motorcyclist, who wears the rubberised motorcycle leather coat and aviator goggles.

Two photographs taken in sequence showing a Nord artillery company during an offensive operation in the summer of 1941. The men can be seen manhandling a 7.5cm le.IG18 light infantry gun. Although the gun was one of the first post-First World War weapons to be issued, it remained in service throughout the war. The gun was light and robust, employed a shotgun breech action, and was well liked among SS gunners.

A photograph of SS gunners with their 10.5cm le.FH18 howitzer in its firing position in a field being readied for action. Normally there were four guns in a battery, but depending on losses or the strength of the enemy the battery was occasionally consolidated into slightly larger batteries. The 10.5cm howitzer had either an eight- or a nine-man crew.

In summer camouflage an MG gunner is seen during a lull in the fighting taking a well-earned cigarette. In 1941 the SS were organized into three regimental units, each of them consisting of three battalions with three infantry companies and one heavy company. The infantry companies were all motorized and armed with three light mortars, two heavy and nine light machine guns. The heavy weapons company consisted of six mortars and eight heavy machine guns.

Two photographs showing a German crossing point in one of the numerous rivers and lakes during the German advance on Murmansk in 1941. The soldiers of an unidentified unit are seen moving vehicles and armour across a river using sections of a pontoon bridge which are being towed by an inflatable boat with outboard motor. Throughout the war the German soldier's ingenuity to use various modes of transportation was unceasing, and this helped him retain and often regain the initiative on the battlefield.

An 8cm sGrW 34 mortar crew during a fire mission inside a forested area. The design of this weapon was conventional and it broke down into three loads (barrel, bipod, baseplate) for transport. The 8cm GrW 34/1 was an adaptation for use in self-propelled mountings.

A photograph showing a reconnaissance patrol. The undergrowth gives these men good cover against detection and their spotted camouflage smocks blend in well with the local terrain.

Six photographs taken in sequence showing Nord infantryman during an attack against Soviet troops inside a forested area during the division's advance towards Murmansk in the summer of 1941. Note the barbed wire entanglements that the Russians have erected to hinder German movement through the forest. Fighting in closed areas such as forests was often hazardous for the soldiers. The dense vegetation limited lines of sight and fire, and the terrain, often without good roads, was frequently inaccessible to vehicles, which made supply and transport difficult. The problems of transport made engineering resources increasingly important, and as a result pioneers were drafted in to improve roads and build bridges and airfields. The forest environment, in both summer and winter, could be inherently unhealthy, with the danger of various diseases. The terrain could also make it difficult to deploy armoured forces, or any other kind of forces on any large scale. The Germans quickly learned that to fight successfully in the forests of northern Russia effective small unit tactics and leadership were essential. On the other hand, they also learned that the forest could be their ally, with opportunities for camouflage and plenty of material with which to build bunkers, fortifications and other forms of protection.

An MG34 light machine gun crew wearing their winter whites have halted in the snow. One of the most important factors in overwhelming the enemy was when Soviet forces faced a well supplied machine gun team with plenty of ammunition.

A good photograph showing the effects of a flamethrower hitting a target inside a forest. The flamethrower, though deadly, remained rare within the SS during the early phase of the war on the eastern front. Limitations of production and tactical applicability restricted its use.

Gunners belonging to the 1 Kompanie of Regiment 11 can be seen with their light 7.5cm le.IG18 infantry gun which is defending a road junction inside a forest clearing in the summer of 1941. Note the wicker ammunition cases which have been opened and some of the projectiles stacked for firing.

Two photographs showing Wehrmacht, Finnish and Nord troops crossing a pontoon bridge during their advance in the Kiestinki area. Fighting in the region had been moderate and losses to the SS regiments low. The area comprised many lakes, rivers, swamps and other waterways in the most northern regions of Russia. Troop movement was often hindered by water which was a natural barrier for the Red Army defending the area. Nonetheless, German pioneers were drafted in to erect pontoon bridges. In the second photograph pioneers can be seen on the river bank with a bridging section.

Animal draught towing supplies can be seen crossing a pontoon bridge in September 1941. Throughout the war the German army used animal draught extensively to move supplies, armour and manpower from one part of the front to another.

A Horch cross-country car and other vehicles that are camouflaged by saplings are being ferried across a river. By September 1941 Kampfgruppe Nord had received around 700 Waffen-SS troop replacements, which had been attached to the Finnish III Corps operating in the Kiestinki area.

A Gebirgs soldier is seen here in the Kiestinki area in late October 1941 trying to relieve a vehicle that has become stuck in the mud. With the roads nothing more than dirt tracks, vehicles quickly became mired in the mud when there was a downpour. When the first snow showers arrived that month, much of the road system ground to a halt.

Two Nord soldiers can be seen in the snow during winter operations in 1942. They both retain their summer camouflage smocks, and the man on the right is wearing a woollen toque under his M35 helmet and woollen mittens.

Two photographs taken in sequence during an operation in the Kiestinki-Louhi region in November 1941 showing an MG34 machine gun crew with their weapon attached to a Lafette 34 sustained-fire mount with optical sight. Note the special pads on the front of the tripod. These were specifically used when the weapon was being carried on a soldier's back. The pads would allow the carrier some reasonable comfort. Each infantry battalion contained an MG Kompanie, which fielded eight MG34 heavy machine guns on the sustained fire-mount. A heavy machine gun squad usually consisted of six men.

(**Opposite, above**) Pioneers are seen building a wooden crossing over a frozen river during winter operations in 1942. Because of the large numbers of rivers and streams encountered by Nord during its advance all kinds of bridging and river crossings were essential if they were to successfully achieve their objectives.

(**Above**) Infantrymen struggle to free a vehicle stuck in the snow along a road during an operation. Many hours were spent trying to haul stranded vehicles or artillery pieces through the snow. The terrible road system had seriously delayed the German advance, and the Russian winter virtually paralysed it.

(**Opposite, below**) A soldier struggles through the snow with his horse towing a sled full of wood. Using a sled was one of the most effective means of moving infantry equipment from one part of the battlefront to another in the Arctic Circle.

(**Opposite**) Two photographs taken in sequence showing a Nord artillery unit in the snow. The artillerymen are seen next to a 7.5cm GebG36, which was the standard artillery piece used by the mountain troops during the war in the east. There were normally four or five of these guns in a mountain battery. They were well-liked by its crews. The gun had a split trail and the recoil system was a variable system that automatically shortened the recoil as the elevation increased. The disc wheels were lightweight with solid rubber tyres, though some had wood-spoke wheels. There was no splinter shield due to the fact that the gun was primarily designed for mountain use. This helped to keep the weight down and enabled the whole weapon to be broken down into eight loads relatively quickly.

(**Above**) An injured Nord soldier is being accompanied by his comrade back to a field dressing station following an enemy contact along the front in the winter of 1942. Both men are wearing the white winter camouflage suits which have become soiled with mud and grime following days and weeks of combat.

An SS Nord squad or platoon leader during a pause in his unit's march has a much-needed cigarette. He is wearing a summer camouflage smock and has moved his mosquito net around to the side of his head. Note his ammunition pouches for a 9mm MP40 machine pistol. These pouches were able to hold three 32 rounds of ammunition.

(**Opposite, above**) A Nord outpost during an enemy contact in the winter of 1942. These troops can be seen moving along a position. Often the front was a mass of trenches, fortifications with mines, barbed wire entanglements, and basic slit trenches known by the Germans as a Stichgraben.

(**Opposite, below**) An 8cm Nord mortar crew can be seen moving forward through the snow. The weapon was of conventional design and was broken down into three loads: the smooth bore barrel which can be seen being carried by this leading soldier on his shoulder, a bipod, and base plate. Attached to the bipod was a traversing hand-wheel and a cross-levelling hand-wheel below the elevating mechanism. A panoramic sight was mounted on the traversing mechanism yoke for adjustments.

A Nord Pak crew in action with their 3.7cm PaK35/36. Even though the PaK35/36 had become inadequate for operational needs in the face of growing armoured opposition, they were still quite capable of causing serious damage.

Chapter Two

The Kestenga Front 1942–43

The plan was for the invasion of the Soviet Union to be won within four months, before the winter. But the generals had underestimated the vastness of the country and the resilience of the Soviet people. By October 1941 it was clear to the German planners that the war they were fighting was not going to be won by winter. What mattered to the soldiers in the far north of Russia was keeping warm. When the first snow fell on the Kestenga front in early October 1941 Nord troops found themselves without warm, protective clothing, and they had to quickly improvise. Many relied on Finnish winter stocks, fur boots and animal skin coats along with padded winter white ski suits. Those that relied on German winter clothes made crude attempts to keep themselves warm and camouflage themselves in the snow. This meant draping a single white sheet over their uniforms. While it afforded some degree of camouflage in the snow, it did not keep the wearer very warm.

Another early attempt was the use of the snow shirt, the two-piece snow suit and the single-piece snow overall. During the first winter period there were a number of winter uniforms hastily put into service.

Life for the Nord Division in the forests, marshes, and frozen lakes that surrounded the Kestenga region was tough. The German soldiers had great respect for the Finns who supported them and gave them practical ideas for staying alive in the winter, including the building of igloos and a multitude of other constructions.

Masses of trenches and defensive positions were erected along the front as the troops would spend considerable amounts of time in static front lines.

Elsewhere on the German northern front troops fought a series of bloody battles to hold their positions around Leningrad. Although they had managed to blunt Russian penetrations through their lines, they had sacrificed thousands of men killed and wounded. The battles had absorbed all the available resources of the 18th Army and elements of the 11th, and the planned assault on Leningrad being abandoned. As a consequence of this, the whole front came to a grinding halt and a sense of futility and gloom gripped the German soldier in the north.

As the spring thaw arrived in 1942 most units were substantially in the same position they had been at the end of 1941. From the Volkhov River to the Gulf of

Finland the front was reminiscent of the First World War – with a string of trenches and shell holes in which gains and losses could be measured in yards. As a result of defeats in southern Russia, German forces were now compelled to go on the defensive against growing resistance. Despite the prevailing conditions and the daily shelling, Leningrad gradually regained strength and became a fortress capable of withstanding a further year and a half of siege and every enemy attempt to destroy it. Costly as this defence was, it managed to pin down large parts of Army Group North which were desperately needed elsewhere.

In June 1942 Nord Division was upgraded to the SS Gebirgsjäger Nord Division. They participated in static combat conducting long-range patrols, raids and defensive attacks against numerous Soviet offensives. Much of the land over which they fought was mosquito-infested forests with swamps, cut by waterways and tracks running through the undergrowth. Men of the Nord Division were totally aware of the geographical significance of the area and its swamps, which acted as a natural obstacle. The Germans had established quite a large and strongly defended bridgehead covering a huge area of territory running up to the borders with Finland. Along the front, well armed German soldiers held firm, determined not to give one inch to the Red Army.

In August 1942 the Nord Division was withdrawn from the front and transported to Finland for a rest and refit. Here it was again re-designated, this time as the SS-Gebirgs-Division Nord Waffen-SS Norwegian Freiwilligen. It was replenished with more well trained soldiers, given additional weapons, and, under the command of Gust Jonassen, began forming an elite ski unit. The ski recruits were transferred to Alsace for training. Although few had military experience, most showed themselves to be very competent skiers. While infantry training progressed at a number of locations, officer candidates, including Jonassen, went through the SS officer school at Bad Tölz in Bavaria.

In late winter 1942 the Nord Division was back on the Kestenga front, ready for action. From its positions it continued patrols and fighting skirmishes with Russian troops.

In February 1943 the SS-Freiwilligen-Schikompanie Norge was attached to the division. This unit was a group of volunteers of Norwegians, Swedes and Danish expert skiers under the command of Jonassen. Their primary task was to advance across the snow at speed to conduct patrols and implement ambushes. They had been expertly trained not only to ski, but to climb and endure long marches, survive appalling conditions, and they were given a role as crack shock troops. Yet, as with the German mountain or Gebirgs troops, they often had little opportunity to demonstrate their unique skills. Instead, these elite ski troops were employed mainly as assault infantry in conventional battle, a role in which they excelled, but not one for which they had been trained.

The SS-Freiwilligen-Schikompanie Norge supported the main units of the Nord Division very successfully. However, its service was short-lived. Apart from suffering a number of casualties, including Jonassen who stepped on a mine in May 1943 and was replaced by Otto Andreas Holmen, the unit was withdrawn to Norway and then back to Finland, ending its service with Nord.

During operations in 1942 and a Nord ski patrol are seen wearing the one-piece camouflage snow suit over their uniforms. Most of the men are carrying over their shoulder the Kar98k carbine bolt action rifle, which was distributed to all infantrymen during the war. Note two soldiers with the ready-to-use 50-round MG34 machine gun belts draped around their necks.

(**Above**) A ski patrol departs from a village wearing the familiar two-piece camouflage snow suit. They can clearly be seen wearing the coloured friend-or-foe recognition stripes on both sleeves. Two of the troops are armed with a whitewashed MP40 machine gun, while the remainder are carrying the Kar98k bolt action rifles.

(**Opposite, above**) Out in the snow and a soldier is seen with dogs pulling a sled. In order to camouflage him in the snow he wears the snow overall. The snow overall was worn without a belt over the uniform and equipment. It was produced in large numbers and issued to the mountain troops and the Nord division, but it did not prove to be as practical as other camouflage smocks as it tended to restrict the wearer's freedom of movement.

(**Opposite, below**) Soldiers are seen here using a sled to move from one part of the front to another. In 1942 most motive power of the infantry divisions was animal draught. Many hundreds of thousands of horses died, sometimes thousands in a day, either due to combat action, the extreme weather, lack of forage, or they were eaten by starving soldiers.

Two photographs taken in sequence of the same column.

Troops during a ski patrol. Most of the soldiers are wearing the two-piece snowsuit comprising a snow jacket and matching trousers. The jacket was buttoned all the way down the front with white painted buttons. It had a large white hood which could easily be pulled over the steel helmet. The hood not only helped conceal the headgear if it had not already received any type of winter covering, but also afforded protection to the back of the wearer's neck and to the ears. The trousers were often tucked into the boots.

(**Above**) Two photographs taken in sequence showing a Nord soldier in a local defence role with his MG34 machine gun which is mounted on an anti-aircraft tripod mount. Throughout the war support units were issued with light machine guns for self-defence and were able to counter low-flying enemy aircraft. This machine gunner wears the animal skin fur coat issued to German troops driving vehicles or on guard duties on the eastern front during the winter.

(**Opposite & following**) Eight photographs showing an SS Division Nord ski patrol during operations in Army Group North during the winter of 1942. They are all wearing the early winter camouflage smocks over their uniforms and fur-covered head-dress. The fur covered caps were issued to troops serving in the east during the winter of 1942. Most of the men are carrying the Kar98k carbine bolt action rifle.

A ski patrol in deep snow during operations in northern Russia in 1942. Signs of enemy movement were easier to identify in the snow, and a vigilant patrol could quickly detect the location of their enemy by fresh footprints or snow knocked off bushes.

A ski trooper on a reconnaissance mission armed with a captured Russian Tokarev rifle. Note that the trooper's binoculars are protected by a knitted woollen cover. This was done not to camouflage the binoculars, but to protect the relatively fragile working parts from the extreme cold.

These ski troops are on patrol and are all wearing the shapeless two-piece snowsuit. With Red Army soldiers wearing similar clothing, front-line German troops were issued with coloured arm bands for use on their winter clothing so they could distinguish between friend and foe.

An injured soldier is being moved by sled across the snow.

(**Above**) Ski troops seen during a reconnaissance mission. Skis were a very effective means of movement across the frozen terrain and were used extensively by reconnaissance patrols. The division had initially fought poorly, but after training with Finnish troops it became a highly effective unit, often serving alongside the army's 7th Gebirgsjäger Division.

(**Opposite**) Two photographs showing ski troops on a patrol. They can be seen moving forward on the snow. Ski troops were particularly effective against enemy formations, appearing suddenly out of the snow to sweep across a trench line, attacking the position, disappearing back across the snow and returning to its lines.

During a lull in the fighting along the front and a mortar crew takes time out to have a cigarette. They are all wearing the two-piece snowsuit and their steel helmets have received an application of whitewash for camouflage.

(**Opposite, above**) A group of ski troops is halted near a line of trees in the snow. The soldiers are armed with a variety of weapons, including Kar98K bolt-action rifles, MP40 sub-machine guns and a captured Tokarev rifle. The MP40 was used extensively by ski troops. They were less of a burden than rifles while skiing and they could be brought into action more quickly.

(**Opposite, below**) Ski troops preparing to move from one part of the front to another using sleds and animal draught to transport supplies. In the far north of Russia wheeled transport was generally useless in the trackless wastes and forests, and almost invariably the most effective means of transport was by sled.

(**Above**) Troops gather their personal equipment before resuming their mission across the snow. Soldiers found moving through snow on foot was particularly difficult in many areas and quite exhausting. As a consequence, much of the movement in the snow was undertaken using skis and sleds.

(**Opposite, above**) A heavy MG34 mounted on the Lafette 34 sustained fire-mount. The squad is well concealed and their uniforms blend in well with the local snowy terrain. This MG34 Lafette had a telescopic sight and special sighting equipment for indirect fire. Another important feature of this weapon was that the legs could be extended to allow it to be used in the anti-aircraft role, and when lowered it could be placed to allow the gun to be fired remotely or aimed through a periscope attached to the tripod. It was a very successful gun and used extensively until the end of the war. In defensive positions, which became more familiar by mid-1943, the MG34 Lafette could hold up entire enemy units for hours or days. They were deadly weapons and the Russians attacked them with caution.

(**Opposite, below & following**) Five photographs taken in sequence showing the rare sight of seeing ski soldiers building an igloo. Under extreme arctic conditions it was vital to bring every man under cover at night, and guard duty was limited to short periods. The igloos the men constructed, which had initially been done under the training and supervision of the Finns, had a number of positive advantages: being made of snow they were naturally camouflaged, and their thick walls were wind-proof and provided insulation against the cold. The igloos were adapted by the soldiers and used as defensive positions as seen in one photograph showing an MG34 machine gunner and rifleman.

A Nord soldier with a mule. The mule would be the main source of transporting equipment to the front across rugged and mountainous terrain. These hardy pack animals were better suited for rough terrain than horses and were used extensively by the mountain soldiers throughout the war.

(**Opposite, above**) Signalmen using lightweight radio sets. These portable radio sets were widely used during the war and could be carried in two parts by the radiomen on specially designed back-pack frames. This ski patrol is more than likely part of a reconnaissance unit at a forward observation post, where they are obtaining details of enemy movements and sending back the information via radio to divisional headquarters.

(**Opposite, below**) A whitewashed Pz.Kpfw.III with a number of Nord and regular troops who have hitched a lift onboard the tank and are seen moving along a snowy track flanked by infantry on foot. Note the horseshoe attached to the vehicle to bring the crew good luck.

An observer during a reconnaissance mission in Finland looks through a pair of periscope binoculars. Given the generic name of Scherenfernrohr, or 'scissor' binoculars, these were manufactured primarily by Leitz, but were also made by Zeiss. They were used as rangefinders and were mounted on a tripod S.F.14.Z.Gi. Each artillery battery had an observation post among the frontline positions. In extreme conditions the lenses sometimes iced over hampering surveillance of the front lines.

(**Opposite, above**) A soldier from the 7th Gebirgsjäger Division is seen leading a horse-drawn sled with a Nord soldier bound for the front line. Horses often carried or pulled considerable quantities of equipment. The troops often had to carry several days rations and equipment.

(**Opposite, below**) A column of ski troops advance across the frozen Russian terrain accompanied by horse-drawn sledges. Fighting against the Red Army could be fierce one moment, suffering lots of casualties, and then the front could suddenly grind to a halt for many days without firing a shot.

A Nord ski trooper armed with a captured whitewashed Tokarev rifle. One sub-machine gun to be found in the German arsenal was the popular PPSh-41, which was regarded as more reliable than the MP40 in winter conditions.

(**Opposite, above**) During a night-time patrol and these ski troops can be seen moving across the snow. Behind them a number of buildings have been set ablaze following some heavy contact with the enemy.

(**Opposite, below**) Sitting on a mound of snow, two ski troops pose for the camera. Note the soldier on the left wearing the German version of the Soviet-style felt boots. Both men are wearing their white snow overalls which were excellent for use while skiing.

(**Above**) Nord soldiers during a pause in their march converse and have a cigarette. Note the soldier on the left displaying some of his personal kit including a black leather belt and rifle ammunition pouches for his Karabiner 98K. Note the man standing behind the soldiers – he was more than likely a 'helper' assisting the troops.

(**Opposite, above**) Two Nord soldiers surveying the area ahead. The rifleman is armed with a captured Soviet SVT-40 Tokarev self-loading rifle. There were popular trophies with both German and Finnish troops. They were accurate and their semi-automatic action gave them a much higher rate of fire than the standard German issue bolt-action Mauser.

(**Opposite, below**) Here in this photograph, which is probably a posed shot, as otherwise the photographer would have been risking his life, ski troops are spread out across the snow with their weapons at the ready.

A posed photograph of a ski trooper. Nord took part in many defensive operations in northern Finland near Kiestinki where it fought alongside the Finnish Army III Corps. From 1943 the division saw action in the province of Karelia and fought shoulder to shoulder with members of the 7th Gebirgsjäger Division.

(**Opposite, above**) A Nord soldier armed with the MP38/40 sub-machine gun during a fire mission against an enemy target. The specialist nature of their work often meant that these mountain troops of the SS cooperated well with regular Heer troops, unlike the hostility so often the norm between more conventional army and SS units. The men of Nord Division worked closely with the 7th Gebirgsjäger Division, which spent much of the war based in Lapland. A number of photographs in this volume show evidence of this cooperation.

(**Opposite, below**) An interesting photograph showing a heavy MG34 machine gun on a sustained-fire mount in the snow, flanked by ski troops with their weapons at the ready. In open terrain such as this, an MG34 machine gun squad would use their sustained fire-mount to protect the flanks of the advancing rifle companies. However in built-up areas the crews often had to operate forward with the rifle platoons and in light machine gun roles with bipods only. They were still able sometimes to take advantage of the situation and revert back to a heavy machine gun role.

(**Above**) Troops are seen preparing to transport an injured soldier across the snow on a sled. Along some of the front the Germans found there was no main battle line, no outposts, and no reserves, just small groups of troops depending on each other to hold defended areas. Life across much of the front was at a standstill and those troops that went out on reconnaissance missions regularly clashed with Red Army units, frequently sustaining casualties.

(**Opposite, above**) A unit belonging to the 7th Gebirgsjäger Division can be seen crossing a river during operations in Finland. The division spent the entire war in the Lapland region of the far north and supported the Nord Division until the Axis pulled out of the region back into Norway. The division stayed in Norway until it surrendered to the British in May 1945.

(**Opposite, below**) Nord ski troopers returning from a reconnaissance patrol inside a wooded area. Note one of the soldiers wearing the distinctive sheepskin line grey winter anorak with fur hood. His reversible trousers are grey-side out and are tucked into a pair of short shaft ski-boots. He has a general issue Kar98k rifle slung over his back for ease of carriage while marching.

Two photographs showing men of the Nord Division with the 99th Pioneer Abteilung and parts of the 99th Division support unit of the 7th Gebirgsjäger Division. In the first photograph pioneers can be seen with a bridging section being transported along a muddy road. The other photograph shows Nord troops watching the pioneers and support units putting together the bridging section across a river.

Nord troops during a reconnaissance mission come across a deserted Russian position. Both the Red Army and the Germans had many hundreds of miles of defensive positions that comprised arrays of bunkers, machine gun and anti-tank defences, barbed wire entanglements, or areas of holes and ditches where soldiers spent days or weeks encamped.

The graves of two Nord soldiers. Losses by the Nord Division steadily grew throughout the war.

(**Opposite, above**) A group of Nord soldiers can be seen conversing in a town that has been razed by Soviet bombing. The Russian attacks were designed to deny the Germans any shelter and keep them exposed. As such, troops could be easily spotted by reconnaissance aircraft, and suffered as a result.

(**Opposite, below**) Two Pz.Kpfw.IIs can be seen passing pioneers attached to the SS Gebirgs-Division Nord in 1942. The area can be seen totally devastated by either heavy artillery or air bombardments. This type of tactical bombardment was all very well, but during the winter the lack of shelter was often problematic for the soldiers.

(**Above**) Soldiers of the SS Gebirgs-Division Nord stand beside two stationary Pz.Kpfw.II tanks during operations on the Kestenga front. The soldier standing to the left of the motorcyclist, who is wearing the special motorcycle protective suit, appears to be armed with a captured Russian 7.62mm Mosin-Nagant M1891/30 rifle. The Germans designated this Soviet weapon as the Gew252(r).

A crossing point has been established and Nord troops with a motorcycle combination from an unidentified unit use inflatable boats. Inflatable boats could be put into operation much quicker than a pontoon bridge and were less vulnerable to attack.

Nord soldiers were often employed as assault infantry or as long-range reconnaissance patrollers. Here in some woods, troops gather to discuss their next movement. Note they are wearing the distinctive SS summer camouflage smocks with M43 field cap. Camouflaged field caps were manufactured but were not as widely issued.

Chapter Three

Withdrawal from Finland

In July 1943 the front-line German strength in Army Group North was 710,000 men. The army was also building up huge reserves echeloned in depth behind the northern fronts in Estonia and Latvia. The Germans and Soviets in northern Russia were almost equal in strength, but the Red Army were known to have even greater reserves. They were also building up significant forces around Leningrad and Nevel. The Germans shifted Luftwaffe, Wehrmacht and SS units to strengthen their lines.

Further north Division-Nord saw only minor enemy activities, but morale was low and illness high. Mosquitoes continued to plague the men. From their bunkers and makeshift wooden structures the soldiers patrolled, but seldom engaged in heavy fighting.

All Waffen-SS divisions were numbered according to formation dates, and in October Nord became known as the 6th SS Gebirgs-Division Nord – the title they would hold until the end of the war.

By the end of 1943 the German tactical position in Army Group North had become fragile. This was made worse on 14 January 1944 when the Red Army launched its winter offensive against the Leningrad and Volkhov Fronts. The German 18th Army were outnumbered by least 3:1 in divisions, 3:1 in artillery, and 6:1 in tanks, self-propelled artillery, and aircraft.

By the morning of 18 January the fronts east of Oranienbaum and west of Leningrad were collapsing. The same was happening at Novgorod where a number of German units were being encircled. The Russian Second Shock and Forty-Second Armies then joined the attack against Army Group North. Along the Baltic coast some German elements escaped, but many were trapped and destroyed as the Russians swept in from the east and west. At Novgorod eight Soviet divisions encircled five German battalions. Their one hope of avoiding annihilation was to escape and hide in the swamps west of the city.

As Novgorod was pulverized into oblivion by Russian artillery, the Forty-Second Army attacked toward Krasnogvardeysk and started battering German units defending the town. The 18th Army was beginning to disintegrate. Fighting in mud and swampland, the troops were exhausted. On 23 January Pushkin and Slutsk were evacuated. General Kuechler, the new commander of Army Group North, appealed to Hitler for a complete withdrawal, but Hitler prohibited all voluntary withdrawals and reserved all decisions to withdraw to himself. One week later, after the 18th Army had incurred more than 50,000 casualties, Hitler approved a retreat to the Luga River but directed that the front be held, contact with 16th Army regained, and all gaps in the front closed.

For the next few months the German front held as the Russians built up their reserves for a new offensive. The Germans tried their best to bring additional reinforcements to the area, and although the temporary lull had given them time to build new defensive positions, Army Group North were now exposed to an even greater menace that would now threaten Finland and the Baltic States. With concerns that Finland would soon be overrun by the Red Army the Nord Division prepared defensive positions and planned to evacuate as much materiel as possible from the region in preparation for withdrawal. The German withdrawal from Finland was codenamed Operation Birch.

Further south, in Russia, the German front was experiencing defensive problems in many areas, and in spite of strong fortified positions, which were manned with Pak guns and lines of machine gun pits, the Red Army moved forward in their hundreds regardless of the cost in their own lives.

Already German reserves and reinforcements were dwindling. All along the battered and blasted front German troops tried in vain to hold their positions against overwhelming odds. While a number of areas cracked under the weight of the Russian onslaught, there were many places where German units continued to demonstrate their ability to defend the most hazardous positions against well-prepared and superior enemy forces. Along the front German infantry divisions bitterly contested large areas of countryside. Fighting was often savage, resulting in terrible casualties on both sides.

A change of Finnish leadership in early August 1944 led the Germans to believe that Finland would try to attain a separate agreement with the Russian government. What followed was a Finnish ceasefire that suddenly triggered frantic efforts by the Germans to initiate Operation Birch and begin evacuating men and materiel from southern Finland. With the evacuation in full swing, Finnish forces, which included the 3rd, 6th, and 11th divisions, as well as the 15th and Border Jaeger brigades, were ordered to take up arms against the Germans.

Division Nord formed the rearguard for the three German corps that were withdrawing from Finland. From September to November 1944 it marched over a thousand miles to Mo i Rana in Norway, where it entrained for the southern end of the country. The Norwegian Ski Battalion unit was left behind and merged into the SS-und-Schi-Jäger-Polizei-Battalion 506 (mot.) with a number of personnel from various German police units in southern Norway.

The rest of the Nord Division was then transferred to Denmark where it was briefly refitted. Due to a serious lack of troop reserves the division was replaced by a mixed number of local militia, postal defence units, and Volksdeutsche (ethnic Germans) who were undertrained and badly equipped. Surprisingly, even in the rank and file of this mixed SS division, morale remained high. They needed no propaganda to urge them on and knew that they were fighting now to defend their homes and loved ones. All that what was left to them was their skill and courage. Everything else, guns, planes, and armoured vehicles, had already been sacrificed.

Ski troops on a reconnaissance mission in early 1944. By this period of the war, great pressure was being exerted on German Army Group North. In January the Soviets unleashed a massive winter offensive in which a number of German units were encircled. This put demands on the Nord Division that was in the far north of Russia, and any plans of moving south to support Wehrmacht forces withdrawing towards to the Baltic would now be impossible. Instead, it would continue operating as it had done between Russia and Finland, harassing Soviet attacks and probing enemy lines.

(**Above**) Ski troops wearing winter whites on the march in January 1944. Note the PaK gun being transported on a sled.

(**Opposite, above**) An infantry support vehicle has halted on a road and some of the troops have disembarked. Note the excellent display of an infantryman's combat equipment, which generally consisted of the shelter quarter, canteen, bread bag, gas mask canister and entrenching tool. They also wear the rifleman's ammunition pouches for the general issue Kar98k rifle.

(**Opposite, below**) Troops during a reconnaissance mission are seen. The soldiers can clearly be seen wearing the coloured friend-or-foe recognition stripes on their sleeves. Note how their winter whites have become soiled with dirt and grime.

(**Above**) A rare opportunity to see an Sd.Kfz.251/22 advancing in the snow in northern Russia. This halftrack was armed with a 7.5cm PaK40 L/46 auf Mittlerer Schützenpanzerwagen. Although the gun was too big for the carriage, and overloaded, it was still an effective weapon despite being outdated by 1944. Only a few SS units were seen with these specially adapted halftracks.

(**Opposite, above**) A chance to see a Wehrmacht Sd.Kfz.251/17 anti-aircraft vehicle armed with the 2cm KwK38 on a pedestal mounting with a small armoured turret to protect the gunner. This vehicle is protecting the movement of infantry from enemy aerial attacks in the far north of Russia in the Murmansk region on the Arctic front where Nord was operating.

(**Opposite, below**) A posed photograph showing Nord ski troopers with their rifles at the ready during a fire mission. Note the cuff title bearing the name of Reinhard Heydrich. These soldiers are from the SS-Gebirgsjäger Regiment 11. This was the only unit in the Waffen-SS that bore Heydrich's name.

Another photograph showing the cuff title of Reinhard Heydrich SS-Gebirgsjäger Regiment 11. This regiment was previously formed from the 6th SS Totenkopf-Standarte and SS Infantry Regiment 6, and was given an honorary title by the order of Hitler following the death of Heydrich on 4 June 1942. It is unknown why Hitler bestowed this title on this regiment.

An SS-Gebirgsjäger Regiment 11 'Reinhard Heydrich' soldier can be seen painting slogans on shells before firing them at the enemy during operations in 1944. Over the coming summer months of 1944 the German front in the far north held as the Russians built up their reserves for a new offensive. German units tried their best to bring additional reinforcements to the area to try to hold their positions.

Soldiers preparing to march. Note the excellent display of an infantryman's combat equipment. They wear black ankle boots with canvas gaiters into which their field grey wool trousers are tucked. They are all wearing the M43 field cap and are armed with the bolt action 98k rifle, except one soldier who can be seen with a light MG34. One soldier wears his grey field blouse, but with SS camouflaged pattern trousers. Note that the men are not carrying bulky rucksacks, preferring to carry a blanket roll, often wrapped in a Zeltbahn shelter quarter.

A portrait photograph of a Sturmmann of SS Nord. He wears the standard grey field blouse and his headgear is an M38 field cap with a machine woven SS death's head cap insignia, which was worn on most forms of headgear.

SS Nord soldiers during a parade ceremony in 1944. There are a number of soldiers lined up holding ranks of a Schütze, Sturmmann, Rottenführer, Unterscharführer and Oberscharführer. They all wear the standard field grey field blouse and grey trousers with black ankle boots and black leather belt with field grey painted buckle.

Two officers are seen in a forest during operations in 1944. The terrain in which Nord operated was often dark, damp swampland and forests, as a result of which the division suffered heavy casualties.

An officer watches a Nord soldier climbing onto a pontoon bridge. The SS trooper wears the SS smock with the green summer pattern outermost. His headgear is the M43 field cap which was worn extensively by mountain soldiers during the war.

(**Above**) Support vehicles are seen here arriving at the front during the summer of 1944. The vehicles have been placed on special railway flatcars in order for them to be easily transported off onto the platform.

(**Opposite**) Soldiers are sorting out mail that has arrived from home. By mid-1944 Nord was under considerable pressure as the German front in the east was almost at breaking point. Although fighting in Nord's sector remained relatively stable the Germans were concerned that Finland would soon be targeted by the Red Army. Already, further south, the Baltic States were being threatened, and the Soviets had begun their summer offensive aimed at crushing Army Group Centre.

(**Above**) Supporting regular and Gebirgsjäger units in the Murmansk sector a 2cm flak gun has been mounted on the back of a vehicle and is targeting an enemy aircraft. These flak guns were primarily used during the war for guarding troops in the field, rail lines, bridges and other areas deemed vulnerable to enemy attack.

(**Opposite, above**) An SS Scharführer can be seen cooking over a fire inside a forest in 1944. This mountain trooper wears an SS summer camouflage smock with an SS deaths head cap insignia.

(**Opposite, below**) Soldiers belonging to SS-Nord cross a wooden bridge through a forested area. It was normally down to the special pioneer platoon to erect these bridges to get troops from one part of the battle front to another without hindrance.

Set up on a ridge is a Nord platoon command post. Note the platoon leader, an SS-Untersturmführer, with a field telephone and map. These troops have mosquito nets to combat the insects that constantly plagued the forested and marshy areas of the far north in the summer months.

A rifle squad, some of whom are wearing mosquito nets, are seen on the march. Resting in the clearing are two heavy MG34 guns squads with their weapons on the MG tripod mounts. These weapons are attached to their mounts with extension legs removed.

One of the battalions belonging to SS-Gebirgs Artillery Regiment 6 on the move hauling what appears to be 7.5cm l.IG18 field guns along an uneven forest track. This weapon was used in direct infantry support.

A reconnaissance patrol. This SS-Nord unit, wearing their summer camouflage smocks, wade through the undergrowth. The local terrain gives these men good cover against detection and their spotted smocks blend well with the trees and bushes.

(**Opposite, above**) Nord and Gebirgs troops are seen at the water's edge preparing to board two boats during a mission. Note the troop leader armed with an MP40 machine pistol. A number of the other soldiers can be seen wearing their ammunition pouches for their Karabiner 98K rifle.

(**Opposite, below**) Nord and Gebirgs soldiers in a camp during operations in the summer of 1944. Two of the soldiers are armed with the MP40 machine gun pistol. Note the variation of kit worn by the men.

(**Above**) An interesting photograph showing a Nord motorcyclist halted next to a road waiting for a column of Gebirgsjäger vehicles and troops to pass. By this period of the war, virtually all motorcyclists were used for dispatch purposes to various sections of the front. Motorcycles were versatile machines which could move swiftly across many types of terrain carrying information or small deliveries.

Four photographs taken in sequence showing a Nord soldier holding the rank of SS-Rottenführer being presented with the Iron Cross 2nd Class by his commanding officer. The ribbon with the cross was worn through the tunic's second buttonhole only on the day of presentation. Thereafter, only the ribbon was displayed.

On the same day, the commanding officer presents an Iron Cross 1st Class to a soldier holding the rank of SS-Schütze.

Inside a forest clearing and soldiers from the 6.SS-Gebirgs-Division pose for a group photograph with their mosquito nets temporarily pulled back over their headdresses. Mosquitoes plagued the daily routine of the German soldier.

SS troops pause during operations in the Karelia, where it fought until the Finnish armistice in September 1944. The division then marched on foot nearly one thousand miles through Finland and Norway. It arrived in Denmark in December and was transferred to the Palatinate in western Germany.

Nord troops march towards the banks of a lake carrying ammunition boxes. One of the quickest forms of transportation for units was by boat across the various riverways and lakes that dominated the terrain in the arctic circle.

During Nord's withdrawal, soldiers can be seen standing talking while behind them supplies are being loaded onto boats to be transported across a lake. From September 1944 the division formed the rear guard for the three German corps that were withdrawing from Finland.

Soldiers ferrying supplies across a river. Onboard are loaves of bread, which was a vital part of the dwindling stocks of food supplied to the German forces on the eastern front. An MG34 mounted on an anti-aircraft tripod is being used against possible aerial attack, which was now a constant problem for the units.

Troops appear to be on a boat crossing one of the many lakes or rivers that crisscrossed the forested regions in Finland. In late August and early September 1944, the 6th SS Gebirgs-Division withdrew from Finland in what was known as Operation Birch.

Soldiers are seen on pontoon sections about to be ferried across a lake with supplies in September 1944 during the initial stages of its withdrawal from Finland.

Two Nord soldiers during a pause in their march tuck into their rations. They both are wearing the familiar dotted SS camouflage smocks and M43 field cap. Life for these mountain troops was often gruelling and it was common for men to be overcome by exhaustion in the forests.

A photograph in the winter of 1944 showing a SS-Untersturmführer on the right conversing with his men in the snow. By this period of the war, Nord, as part of XVIII Gebirgskorps, was ordered to take part in the retreat through Lapland into Norway, forming part of the corps' rearguard. In late 1944 it was withdrawn from Norway and shipped to Denmark where it joined regular and Waffen-SS units defending the western front.

Chapter Four

Last Months

In the last months of the war German forces continued to recede across a devastated wasteland. On both the western and eastern fronts, the last agonising moments of the war were being played out. In the east in January 1945 the principal objective of the Red Army was for an all-out assault along the Baltic to crush the remaining under-strength German units that had once formed the apparently invincible Army Group North. It would be these attacks that eventually reduced German-held territory in the north-east to a few small pockets of land surrounding three ports: Libau in Kurland, Pillau in East Prussia and Danzig at the mouth of the River Vistula.

Along the Baltic coast the German defenders continued to try to stall the Russian onslaught with the few weapons and men they still had at their disposal. Every German soldier in Army Group Kurland knew what it meant to be defeated. Not only would the coastal garrisons be cut off and destroyed, but masses of civilian refugees would be prevented from escaping from those ports by sea.

On the western front the situation was equally dire. The German Ardennes Offensive, on which Hitler had pinned much of his hopes, had been lost. But this did not deter Hitler from unleashing one more major offensive on the Western Front. The daring plan was to break through the lines of the US Seventh Army and the French 1re Army in the upper Vosges Mountains and on the Alsatian plain and destroy them. This would open the way for a sub-operation name Dentist or Unternehmen Zahnarzt, a drive into the rear of the US Third Army. The codename for this offensive was Operation North Wind or Unternehmen Nordwind.

The Nordwind offensive comprised three corps of the German 1st Army of Army Group G. The attack initially opened up relatively well, but soon German units met stiff resistance. By 9 January, the XXXIX Panzer Corps was engaged as well, and a week later some seventeen German divisions from Army Group G and Army Group Oberrhein, including the 17th SS Panzergrenadier, 21st Panzer, 25th Panzergrenadier, and the 6th SS Gebirgs Division Nord were engaged in the fighting to try to help stabilize the deteriorating situation. Elements of the 6th SS Gebirgs-Division Nord were thrust into the line in a drastic attempt to hold back the advancing Allies in the Vosges region. Though these Waffen-SS mountain troopers were now well seasoned veterans from the eastern front, the offensive was doomed from the start. Nonetheless, supported by the 2nd Gebirgs-Division, the Nord-Division pressed home its attacks and caused severe damage to a number of American units. Although the Americans were superior in both armour and infantry, they were masters at fighting in the surrounding pinewoods. The Alpine skills of the mountain troops unnerved the American troops and in some sectors reduced their fighting abilities. SS Gebirgs Regiment 12 and 506th Battalion which was attached to the 361st Volksgrenadier Division saw extensive action against the US 45th Infantry Division.

For nearly a week the SS troops fought in and around the town of Wingen. Slowly and systematically US soldiers fought their way through the town against SS and Volksgrenadier troops who either fought to the death or escaped the impending slaughter by withdrawing to another makeshift position. Fighting around the town had been a fierce contest of attrition, and although the Germans had showed great fortitude and determination, they were constantly hampered by the lack of weapons and manpower. The remaining troops holding out were subjected to merciless ground and aerial bombardments. Unabated fighting continued and losses were massive. The troops who escaped found themselves in open hostile countryside with American gunners inflicting terrible casualties on them. All that was left was a hard cadre of SS men determined to resist at all costs.

By the second week of January the Nordwind offensive was becoming increasingly desperate. While many areas of the front had cracked under the weight of US strength, a number of German SS units continued to demonstrate their ability to defend the most hazardous positions against well-prepared and greatly superior enemy forces. On 16 January, six companies of the American 157th Infantry Regiment found itself surrounded by SS Regiment 11. Reluctantly, American troops were forced to surrender three days later, losing 482 men. Nord then continued to advance for four more days before being blunted by American counterattacks.

Despite the gradual deterioration in the Nordwind offensive, troops continued to fight on, withdrawing steadily as British and American units advanced towards the Rhine. The Nord division remained on the western front and began organising its units in defensive positions around Trier and Koblenz on the Moselle. Fighting in the area was confusing, and German communication between its various commands was repeatedly lost making the situation worse still. SS and Panzergrenadier soldiers that were embroiled in contact with the enemy for long periods often found that their rear positions had already been evacuated. As a result the troops were regularly exposed to fire without support, and in many cases were encircled and then destroyed. There were many appeals for reinforcements, but most reserves were already embroiled in the defence of Berlin and positioned along the Oder on the eastern front. As a result, most units that were not encircled or tied down in bitter fighting withdrew, all attempting to get through to the main German lines. Morale was reported to be terribly low among the troops. As they endeavoured to break out, they were forced to abandon most of their heavy equipment and weapons. There were frequent scenes of chaos and disorganization along forest roads and paths as they fled from the jaws of the American army. By late March 1945, Division Nord had only 2,000 soldiers left, a mixture of Wehrmacht, Luftwaffe, Volkssturm and Hitlerjugend.

These men attempted to establish defensive lines in the face of the advancing enemy. Their commanders counted on the loyal striking force of Division Nord to hold out for as long as possible, but even the SS were worn down by the constant fighting. A feeling of despair and gloom prevailed. The division withdrew east to re-establish contact with other German units defending the front. However, as it moved, the division was detected by the US Army. What followed in early April 1945 over a period of a week was a series of bitter engagements with the US 71st Division. Division Nord fought doggedly, but American strength soon began overwhelming the Germans.

What was left of the division retreated past Worms, Boppard, across the Rhine and into the German countryside, but American forces finally captured them in May 1945.

Ski troops disembarking from an infantry support vehicle. In the trackless wastes and forests of the north wheeled transport was often useless. The most effective means of transport were usually ski and sled.

An SS-Sturmscharführer, who appears to be drinking a bottle of beer, is flanked by two SS-Untersturmführers.

An SS-Scharführer (second right) is conferring with his men. The man third in from the left is a Finnish soldier. The Finnish Army in 1944 was much as it had been in 1941 – well trained and led but lacking sufficient modern equipment and relying heavily on German weaponry.

(**Above**) A convoy of supply trucks carrying men and equipment has halted along a road. Some of the troops have dismounted from their vehicles and are seen standing near a stream. This is probably a temporary stop before the column resumes its withdrawal.

(**Opposite, above**) In a forest clearing an HF 12 small kitchen wagon can be seen set up and serving warm food. These small mobile kitchens, nicknamed 'goulash cannons', could operate on the move, cooking stews, soups, and coffee. The limber carried utensils and equipment.

(**Opposite, below**) A unit pauses in its march next to a lake in Finland. The division's withdrawal was long and arduous. It generally had no armoured support, and the tanks they did have were invariably French Beutepanzers. Armoured cars were also limited to a few Sd.Kfz.221s, SdkFz.261s and halftracks, some of which mounted flak guns for support. On the other hand, weapons such as mortars and artillery were abundant.

(**Opposite**) Two photographs showing soldiers that have used shelter quarters for housing troops. These field tents were of standard design and had a fly tarp erected over them to provide insulation from the hot sun. They could be quickly erected by the troops, and doing so was part of their training. Without adequate shelter in the arctic regions a soldier might easily die of the cold.

(**Above**) SS and Gebirgs troops are seen on a road in early 1945. An SS-Unterscharführer appears to be holding a map and conferring with a Heeres Gebirgs soldier. The division had withdrawn through Finland and Norway, arrived in Denmark in December 1944, and then transferred to the Palatinate in western Germany.

(**Opposite, above**) Nord soldiers from a lake's edge watch inflatable boats crossing the water. A couple of the men wear mosquito nets over their headgear. All the men are armed with the Karabiner 98K bolt action rifle.

(**Above**) Soldiers carry a wounded comrade on a stretcher to one of the hastily erected field dressing stations in the area. Losses to the division were high, especially during its withdrawal from Finland as it fought in a vicious rearguard action to allow three German corps to retreat.

(**Opposite, below**) Troops pass a burning building in Germany during the last months of the war. By 1945 Nord had lost so many soldiers that the division received a complement of young Volksdeutsche conscripts. They had received only brief training and were ordered by the SS to stand and fight. Their losses were high.

Nord troops pass SS graves during the last months of the war. Following heavy losses in the Nordwind operation in 1945, what was left of the division was used in a static defence near Bitche in February. It was then transferred to the Saar in March where it was almost destroyed. Remnants then fought on with elements from the 38th SS Grenadier Division Nibelungen, until it finally surrendered.

Appendix One

Division-Nord Winter Uniforms

By October 1941, it had become perfectly clear to the Nord Division that the war they were fighting on the Eastern Front was not going to be won by the time winter had set in. The German high command had not anticipated a long-drawn-out battle and predicted in its planning that the war would be won by October at the latest. Consequently they had not planned to combat the Russian winter and it soon became apparent that the vehicles, equipment and clothing with which the German army was supplied were inadequate and inferior to those in service with the Russian Army.

When the first snow showers fell in early October 1941, soldiers were compelled to improvise. The dead of both sides were stripped of overcoats, fur hats and boots, particularly Russian felt boots which afforded the best protection in arctic conditions. The German leather boot afforded protection during short periods of bad weather, but over time soldiers found that they retained the damp, and constant exposure to snow and wet caused them to fall apart. This allowed the socks to become exposed or wet and caused cases of frostbite. Soldiers began lining their boots with straw or paper, if they could find those materials.

Apart from the low temperatures, they also had to consider camouflage. In the winter of 1941/42 soldiers made early attempts to camouflage themselves with white cloth covers. They had crude shapeless white sheets which they draped over their steel helmets and secured in place with the helmet's rubber ring. The sheet was then normally wrapped around the wearer's head and secured by a pin or metal hook beneath the chin. The remainder of the sheet was draped around the arms and upper body and fastened again by another single pin or metal hook on the front to camouflage the service uniform. However it did not allow wearers to move as freely as they would have liked and it limited access to personal equipment, especially under combat conditions. As a result soldiers unfastened the sheet and allowed it to flow, thus reducing the camouflage effectiveness.

Another early attempt by the Nord Division to camouflage themselves during winter operations was the snow shirt. This was a rather tight-fitting design and was pulled over the wearer's head. It had no collar but had long sleeves. The snow shirt had been purposely made long with the shirt-tails reaching down to the wearer's ankles. They were popular: the soldier blended well with the local terrain and was able to move more freely than with the snow sheet. The wearer's personal equipment too was worn outside the garment and this allowed him easy access to it.

During this period soldiers were also issued with the snow overall. It was similar in design to the snow shirt, but not tight-fitting. It was a shapeless long overall garment, buttoned from the neck to the crotch, with a deep collar, and, for the first time, an attached hood and long sleeves. It was generally liked among the soldiers in terms of concealment, but it soon proved not to be a practical item, as it tended to restrict the wearer. It had one major disadvantage that if the trousers needed to be removed, the entire overall had to be undone and completely taken off.

By 1942 manufacturers were designing more practical winter camouflage garments. One item to be produced was the first two-piece snowsuit. It was a shapeless two-piece snowsuit comprising of a snow jacket and matching trousers. The jacket was buttoned all the way down the front with white painted buttons. It had a large white hood which could easily be pulled over the steel helmet. The hood also afforded protection to the back of the wearer's neck and to the ears. The trousers were tucked into the boots.

After the first winter period had been endured there were a number of winter camouflage uniforms hastily put into service. The quality of them varied, but generally they were properly manufactured. In an attempt to restore morale in the troops following the first winter, German High Command produced a handbook on winter warfare and issued it to the troops. Much was made of the morale factor and ways of overcoming the cold weather. It dealt with building shelters, like igloos and various other constructions, and suitable clothing for the winter. It admitted that winter garments, particular those of late 1941, had not reached the front until the worst of the weather had passed, but went on to reassure the reader that there would be adequate winter clothing for future operations, if victory was not attained by then. The winter handbook sought to reassure the soldier that he would not freeze to death in the snow, like so many of his comrades had in late 1941. During the summer of 1942 manufacturers produced hundreds of thousands of winter camouflage uniforms. If the Germans had to fight again in the winter, they would be ready for the weather.

In 1942 a new winter garment was designed, tested and then manufactured. Similar to that worn by the Red Army, it was designed to keep the wearer warm and to provide camouflage in the snow. German troops that wore this uniform during the winter of 1942 tended to wear it for very long periods, both during the day and night. Because of this it became soiled with dirt, thus defeating the purpose of the white camouflage. Soldiers did attempt to clean them but soon found that the thick blanket lining did not clean well or took too long to dry out. For this reason they continued to wear the white camouflage garments already mentioned, as they were easy to clean.

For the winter of 1942 a reversible uniform was supplied to the front lines. When the troops were issued with these garments in October and November 1942, they found them extremely warm and comfortable. They also provided the wearer with greater freedom of movement and access to personal equipment. This uniform also did not cause overheating during physical exertion. It consisted of a heavy reversible double-breasted overjacket designed for extra frontal warmth. It had double-buttoned overlaps to the flaps of the jacket to the front, which when closed were wind-resistant. The bottom edge of the jacket had drawstrings attached, and the ends of the cuffs were adjustable as well. The trousers were thick and also reversible, shorter in length to standard issue trousers but could be worn either over the top of the marching boots or tucked inside. The ends of the trousers could be gathered in by drawstrings. The winter reversible was normally mouse-grey on one side and winter white on the other. If the area was snow covered the wearer wore the uniform on the winter white side out, and where there was no snow, it was worn mouse-grey side out. There were other variations of the reversible, including the green splinter pattern and the tan water pattern. The reversible uniform was designed large enough to be worn over the service uniform, including personal equipment. However troops did favour wearing most of their equipment over the winter jacket.

For the next four years of the war the German soldier was seen wearing these popular winter camouflage garments. By the early winter of 1943, the winter reversible had become one of the most popular items of winter clothing worn by the troops. Soldier survivability increased, in spite of the military setbacks. In the winter of 1941 more than half the casualties were caused by the cold. By the end of 1942 this figure had reduced considerably, and a year later in the winter of 1943 it was less than a quarter.

Had the Germans not so underestimated Russia in 1941, and prepared for a winter war much earlier, then troops would have undoubtedly held the front lines with more success.

Appendix Two

Order of Battle

Order of battle 1941

Division Staff
SS-Infantry Regiments 6 and 7
SS-Infantry Regiment 9 (left the division in December 1941)
SS-Gebirgs Artillery Regiment Nord
SS-Panzerjäger (tank hunter) Battalion Nord
SS-Reconnaissance Battalion Nord
SS-Flak Battalion Nord
SS-Gebirgs Engineer Battalion Nord
SS-Gebirgs Signal Battalion Nord
SS-Division Supply Commander Nord

Order of battle 1942

Division Staff
SS-Gebirgsjäger Regiment 11 'Reinhard Heydrich' with three battalions
SS-Gebirgsjäger Regiment 12 'Michael Gaismair' with three battalions
SS-Infantry Regiment (motorized) 5 (added in 1944)
SS-Skijäger Battalion Norge (a Norwegian volunteer unit)
SS-Gebirgs Artillery Regiment 6 with three artillery groups
SS-Werfer Battalion 6 (rocket artillery)
SS-Gebirgs Panzerjäger Battalion 6 (anti-tank cannons)
SS-Gebirgs Reconnaissance Battalion (motorized) 6
SS-Flak Battalion 6 (anti-aircraft artillery)
SS-Gebirgs Engineer Battalion 6
SS-Gebirgs Signal Battalion 6
SS-Division Supply Commander 6
SS-Feldersatz Battalion 6 (reserve and training battalion)
SS-Sturmgeschütz Battery 6 (assault guns)
SS-Gebirgs-Kriegsberichter Platoon 6 (propaganda platoon)
SS-Feldgendarmerie Platoon 6 (military police)

Appendix Three

Nordwind Order of Battle 1–25 January 1945

1st Army
6th SS Mountain Division
21st Panzer Division
25th Panzergrenadier Division

XIII SS Corps
17th SS Panzergrenadier Division
19th Volksgrenadier Division
36th Volksgrenadier Division

XC Corps
257th Volksgrenadier Division
559th Volksgrenadier Division

LXXXIX Corps
245th Infantry Division
256th Volksgrenadier Division
361st Volksgrenadier Division

German 19th Army
10th SS Panzer Division

LXIV Corps
16th Infantry Division
189th Infantry Division
198th Infantry Division
708th Volksgrenadier Division

LXIII Corps
159th Infantry Division
269th Infantry Division
338th Infantry Division
716th Infantry Division

Appendix Four

Nord Titles & Commanders

Divisional Designated Titles

February – September 1941	SS-Kampfgruppe Nord
September 1941 – September 1942	SS-Division Nord
September 1942 – October 1943	SS-Gebirgs-Division Nord
October 1943 – May 1945	6.SS-Gebirgs-Division Nord

Commanders

February – May 1941	SS-Brigadeführer Karl Herrmann
May 1941 – April 1942	SS-Obergruppenführer Karl-Maria Demelhuber
April 1942	SS-Obergruppenführer Matthias Kleinheisterkamp
April – June 1942	SS-Oberführer Hans Scheider
June 1942 – January 1943	SS-Obergruppenführer Matthias Kleinheisterkamp
January 1943 – June 1944	SS-Gruppenführer Lothar Debes
June – August 1944	SS-Obergruppenführer Friedrich-Wilhelm Krüger
August – September 1944	SS-Brigadeführer Gustav Lombard
September 1944 – April 1945	SS-Gruppenführer Karl Brenner
April – May 1945	SS-Standartenführer Franz Schreiber

Chiefs of Staff

April – June 1941	SS-Hauptsturmführer Joachim Ruoff
June – August 1941	SS-Obersturmbannführer Paul Geiser
August 1941 – April 1942	SS-Sturmbannführer Joachim Ruoff
April – October 1942	SS-Sturmbannführer Eugen Kunstmann
October 1942 – 18 September 1944	SS-Sturmbannführer Heinz Küchle
September 1944 – February 1945	Major Bernhard-Siegfried Sander
March – May 1945	SS-Hauptsturmführer Georg Berger

Appendix Five

Rank Equivalents

German Army	*Waffen-SS*	*British Army equivalent*
Gemeiner, Landser	Schütze	Private
	Oberschütze	
Grenadier	Sturmmann	Lance Corporal
Obergrenadier		
Gefreiter	Rottenführer	Corporal
Obergefreiter	Unterscharführer	
Stabsgefreiter		
Unteroffizier	Scharführer	Sergeant
Unterfeldwebel	Oberscharführer	Colour Sergeant
Feldwebel		
Oberfeldwebel	Hauptscharführer	Sergeant Major
Stabsfeldwebel	Hauptbereitschaftsleiter	
	Sturmscharführer	Warrant Officer
Leutnant	Untersturmführer	Second Lieutenant
Oberleutnant	Obersturmführer	First Lieutenant
Hauptmann	Hauptsturmführer	Captain
Major	Sturmbannführer	Major
Oberstleutnant	Obersturmbannführer	Lieutenant Colonel
Oberst	Standartenführer	Colonel
	Oberführer	Brigadier General
Generalmajor	Brigadeführer	Major General
Generalleutnant	Gruppenführer	Lieutenant General
General	Obergruppenführer	General
Generaloberst	Oberstgruppenführer	
Generalfeldmarschall	Reichsführer-SS	Field Marshal

Notes

Notes

Notes

Notes

Notes